Fix-It and Forget-It®

SWEET & SAVORY SLOW COOKER RECIPES

Fix-It and Forget-It®

SWEET & SAVORY SLOW COOKER RECIPES

48 Appetizers, Soups & Stews, Main Meals, and Desserts

HOPE COMERFORD

Photos by Bonnie Matthews

Good Books books may be purchased in bulk at special discounts for sales promotion, corporate gifts, fund-raising, or educational purposes. Special editions can also be created to specifications. For details, contact the Special Sales Department, Good Books, 307 West 36th Street, 11th Floor, New York, NY 10018 or info@skyhorsepublishing.com.

Good Books is an imprint of Skyhorse Publishing, Inc.®, a Delaware corporation.

Visit our website at www.goodbooks.com.

10 9 8 7 6 5 4 3 2 1

Library of Congress Cataloging-in-Publication Data is available on file.

Cover design by Daniel Brount
Cover photo by Bonnie Matthews

Print ISBN: 978-1-68099-582-4
Ebook ISBN: 978-1-68099-630-2

Printed in China

Table of Contents

Welcome to *Fix-It and Forget-It Sweet & Savory Slow Cooker Recipes*

Are you looking for a tasty weeknight meal you can put together without a lot of fuss, or a sweet treat to surprise your loved ones with? A fun snack for the big game, or a special dessert to bring to a gathering? With this book, a slow cooker, and some easy-to-find ingredients, you'll be all set. From crowd-pleasing appetizers to comforting soups and stews, family-friendly dinners to celebration-worthy desserts, you'll be amazed at all that you and your slow cooker can do. Collected from some of the best home cooks across the country, these recipes are easy to follow and yield results that will impress you and your loved ones. Good cooking doesn't have to be complicated or require you to spend hours in the kitchen. Whether you're making savory snacks, a family dinner, or sweet treats, you may find with these recipes that sometimes simple is best.

Choosing a Slow Cooker

Not all slow cookers are created equal . . . or work equally as well for everyone!

What size slow cooker is best for your household? Here's a quick guide:

For 2–3 person household	3–5 quart slow cooker
For 4–5 person household	5–6 quart slow cooker
For a 6+ person household	6½–7 quart slow cooker

Large slow cooker advantages/disadvantages:

Advantages:

- You can fit a loaf pan or a baking dish into a 6- or 7-quart, depending on the shape of your cooker. That allows you to make bread or cakes, or even smaller quantities of main dishes. (Take your favorite baking dish and loaf pan along when you shop for a cooker to make sure they'll fit inside.)
- You can feed large groups of people, or make larger quantities of food, allowing for leftovers, or meals, to freeze.

Disadvantages:

- They take up more storage room.
- They don't fit as neatly into a dishwasher.
- If your crock isn't ⅔–¾ full, you may burn your food.

Small slow cooker advantages/disadvantages:

Advantages:

- They're great for lots of appetizers, for serving hot drinks, for baking cakes straight in the crock, and for dorm rooms or apartments.
- Great option for making recipes of smaller quantities.

Disadvantages:

- Food in smaller quantities tends to cook more quickly than larger amounts. So keep an eye on it.

- Chances are, you won't have many leftovers. So, if you like to have leftovers, a smaller slow cooker may not be a good option for you.

If you can, have at least two slow cookers; one around 3 to 4 quarts and one 6 quarts or larger. A third would be a huge bonus (and a great advantage to your cooking repertoire!). The advantage of having at least a couple is you can make a larger variety of recipes. Also, you can make at least two or three dishes at once for a whole meal.

Manual vs. Programmable

If you are gone for only six to eight hours a day, a manual slow cooker might be just fine for you. If you are gone for more than eight hours during the day, I would highly recommend purchasing a programmable slow cooker that will switch to warm when the cook time you set is up. It will allow you to cook a wider variety of recipes. Some allow you to set the time in increments of 15 or 30 minutes and some go by 4, 6, 8, or 10 hours.

Get to Know Your Slow Cooker . . .

Plan a little time to get acquainted with your slow cooker. Each slow cooker has its own personality—just like your oven (and your car). Plus, many new slow cookers cook hotter and faster than earlier models. With all of the concern for food safety, the slow cooker manufacturers have amped up their settings so that "High," "Low," and "Warm" are all higher temperatures than in the older models. That means they cook hotter—and therefore, faster—than the first slow cookers. The beauty of these little machines is that they're supposed to cook low and slow. We count on that when we flip the switch in the morning before we leave the house for ten hours or so. So, because none of us knows what kind of temperament our slow cooker has until we try it out, nor how hot it cooks—don't assume anything. Save yourself a disappointment and make the first recipe in your new slow cooker on a day when you're at home. Cook it for the shortest amount of time the recipe calls for. Then, check the food to see if it's done. Or if you start smelling food that seems to be finished, turn off the cooker and rescue your food.

Also, all slow cookers seem to have a "hot spot," which is of great importance to know, especially when baking with your slow cooker. This spot may tend to burn food in that area if you're not careful. If you're baking directly in your slow cooker, I recommend covering the "hot spot" with some foil.

Take Notes . . .

Don't be afraid to make notes in your cookbook. It's yours! Chances are, it will eventually get passed down to someone in your family and they will love and appreciate all of your musings. Take note of which slow cooker you used and exactly how long it took to cook the recipe. The next time you make it, you won't need to try to remember. Apply what you learned to the next recipes you make in your cooker. If another recipe says it needs to cook 7–9 hours, and you've discovered your slow cooker cooks on the faster side, cook that recipe for 6–6½ hours and then check it. You can always cook a recipe longer—but you can't reverse things if it's overdone.

Get Creative . . .

If you know your morning is going to be hectic, prepare everything the night before, take it out of the fridge when you first get up in the morning so the crock warms up to room temperature, then plug it in and turn it on as you're leaving the house.

If you want to make something that has a short cook time and you're going to be gone longer than that, cook it the night before and refrigerate it for the next day. Warm it up when you get home. Or, cook those recipes on the weekend when you know you'll be home and eat them later in the week.

Slow Cooking Tips and Tricks and Other Things You May Not Know

- Slow cookers tend to work best when they're ⅔ to ¾ of the way full. You may need to increase the cooking time if you've exceeded that amount, or reduce it if you've put in less than that. If you're going to exceed that limit, it would be best to reduce the recipe, or split it between two slow cookers. (Remember how I suggested owning at least two or three slow cookers?)

- Keep your veggies on the bottom. That puts them in more direct contact with the heat. The fuller your slow cooker, the longer it will take its contents to cook. Also, the more densely packed the cooker's contents are, the longer they will take to cook. And finally, the larger the chunks of meat or vegetables, the more time they will need to cook.

- Keep the lid on! Every time you take a peek, you lose 20 minutes of cooking time. Please take this into consideration each time you lift the lid! I know, some of you can't help yourself and are going to lift anyway. Just don't forget to tack on 20 minutes to your cook time for each time you peeked!

- Sometimes it's beneficial to remove the lid. If you'd like your dish to thicken a bit, take the lid off during the last half hour to hour of cooking time.

- If you have a big slow cooker (7- to 8-quart), you can cook a small batch in it by putting the recipe ingredients into an oven-safe baking dish or baking pan and then placing that into the cooker's crock. First, put a trivet or some metal jar rings on the bottom of the crock, and then set your dish or pan on top of them. Or a loaf pan may "hook on to" the top ridges of the crock belonging to a large oval cooker and hang there straight and securely, "baking" a cake or quick bread. Cover the cooker and flip it on.

- The outside of your slow cooker will be hot! Please remember to keep it out of reach of children and keep that in mind for yourself as well!

- Get yourself a quick-read meat thermometer and use it! This helps remove the question of whether or not your meat is fully cooked, and helps prevent you from overcooking your meat as well.

    Internal Cooking Temperatures:

    Beef—125–130°F (rare); 140–145°F (medium); 160°F (well-done)

    Pork—140–145°F (rare); 145–150°F (medium); 160°F (well-done)

    Turkey and Chicken—165°F

    Frozen Meat: The basic rule of thumb is, don't put frozen meat into the slow cooker. The meat does not reach the proper internal temperature in time. This especially applies to thick cuts of meat! Proceed with caution!

- Add fresh herbs 10 minutes before the end of the cooking time to maximize their flavor.
- If your recipe calls for cooked pasta, add it 10 minutes before the end of the cooking time if the cooker is on High; 30 minutes before the end of the cooking time if it's on Low. Then the pasta won't get mushy.
- If your recipe calls for sour cream or cream, stir it in 5 minutes before the end of the cooking time. You want it to heat but not boil or simmer.

Approximate Slow Cooker Temperatures (Remember, each slow cooker is different):

High—212°F–300°F

Low—170°F–200°F

Simmer—185°F

Warm—165°F

Appetizers & Snacks

South of the Border Chicken Dip

MARJANITA GEIGLEY, LANCASTER, PA

Makes 28 servings

Prep. Time: 30 minutes ✿ *Cooking Time: 4 hours*
Ideal slow-cooker size: 3-quart

- 1 lb. Velveeta cheese, cubed
- 10-oz. can diced tomatoes and green chilies, drained
- 6 oz. chopped and cooked chicken
- ¼ cup chopped onion
- 1 tsp. cumin
- 2 tsp. cilantro
- 1 dash of Tabasco
- 1 small jar of salsa

1. Combine all ingredients in slow cooker.
2. Cook on Low for 4 hours.

Serve with chips and guacamole.

French Onion Dip

HOPE COMERFORD, CLINTON TOWNSHIP, MI

Makes 6 servings

Prep. Time: 10 minutes *Cooking Time: 8 hours*

Ideal slow-cooker size: 2-quart

2 large sweet yellow onions, finely chopped

4 Tbsp. olive oil

1½ cups plain nonfat Greek yogurt

2 cloves garlic, minced

2 tsp. Worcestershire sauce

¼ tsp. salt

¼ tsp. pepper

Pinch of cayenne

1. Place onions and olive oil in the crock and stir so onions are coated in the olive oil.
2. Cover and cook on Low for 8 hours, or until the onions are a deep caramel brown color.
3. Strain the onions.
4. In a bowl, combine yogurt, garlic, Worcestershire sauce, salt, pepper, cayenne, and onions.

Serve with veggie or potato chips.

Sunday Night Pizza Balls

MARJANITA GEIGLEY, LANCASTER, PA

Makes 10 servings

Prep. Time: 15 minutes *Cooking Time: 2–4 hours*

Ideal slow-cooker size: 7-quart

3 cans (10 per can) Pillsbury® biscuits

1 jar pizza sauce

60 pepperoni slices

30 cubes of Colby cheese

1 beaten egg

2 cups Parmesan cheese

3 Tbsp. Italian seasoning

2 Tbsp. garlic powder

1. Spray slow cooker with nonstick cooking spray.
2. Flatten out each biscuit.
3. Brush pizza sauce on each one.
4. Put pepperoni and cheese on each biscuit.
5. Gather up edges and tuck together.
6. Brush with egg and place in crock.
7. Sprinkle with Parmesan, Italian seasoning, and garlic powder.
8. Cook on Low for 2–4 hours.

TIP

This recipe is a bit labor intensive, but worth the work!

Sweet 'n' Sour Meatballs

VALERIE DROBEL, CARLISLE, PA ✿ SHARON HANNABY, FREDERICK, MD

Makes 15–20 servings

Prep. Time: 10 minutes ✿ *Cooking Time: 2–4 hours*
Ideal slow-cooker size: 3- to 4-quart

12-oz. jar grape jelly

12-oz. jar chili sauce

2 (1-lb.) bags prepared frozen meatballs, thawed

1. Combine jelly and sauce in slow cooker. Stir well.
2. Add meatballs. Stir to coat.
3. Cover and heat on Low 4 hours, or on High 2 hours. Keep slow cooker on Low while serving.

TIP

If your meatballs are frozen, add another hour to your cook time.

Apricot-Glazed Wings

HOPE COMERFORD, CLINTON TOWNSHIP, MI

Makes 8–10 servings

Prep. Time: 30 minutes ❦ *Broiling Time: 16 minutes* ❦ *Cooking Time: 4–6 hours*
Ideal slow-cooker size: 3-quart

4 lb. chicken wings, cut at the joint, tips removed and discarded

salt, to taste

pepper, to taste

garlic powder, to taste

12-oz. jar apricot preserves

¼ cup honey Catalina dressing

2 Tbsp. honey mustard

2 Tbsp. barbecue sauce

1 tsp. lime juice

4 dashes hot sauce

1 small onion, minced

1. Preheat your oven to a low broil.
2. Put your wing pieces onto a baking sheet and sprinkle both sides with salt, pepper, and garlic powder. Put them under the broiler for 8 minutes on each side.
3. While the wings are broiling, mix together the apricot preserves, honey Catalina dressing, honey mustard, barbecue sauce, lime juice, hot sauce, and onion.
4. When your wings are done under the broiler, place them into a greased crock.
5. Pour the sauce you just mixed over the top, then use tongs to toss the wings around to make sure they're all coated with the sauce.
6. Cook on Low for 4–6 hours.

Serve with fresh celery sticks.

Chili Nuts

BARBARA ASTON, ASHDOWN, AR

Makes 5 cups nuts

Prep. Time: 5 minutes *Cooking Time: 2–3 hours*

Ideal slow-cooker size: 3-quart

¼ cup melted butter

2 (12-oz.) cans cocktail peanuts

1⅝-oz. pkg. chili seasoning mix

1. Pour butter over nuts in slow cooker. Sprinkle in dry chili mix. Toss together.
2. Cover. Heat on Low 2–2½ hours. Turn to High. Remove lid and cook 10–15 minutes.

Pesto Tomato Spread

NANCI KEATLEY, SALEM, OR

Makes 12 servings

Prep. Time: 20 minutes ❦ *Cooking Time: 2–3 hours*

Ideal slow-cooker size: 2-quart

2 (8-oz.) pkgs. cream cheese, at room temperature

⅔ cup prepared pesto

3 tomatoes, chopped

½ cup sliced black olives

½ cup chopped fresh basil

1 cup shredded mozzarella

½ cup grated Parmesan cheese

1. Place cream cheese in bottom of lightly greased slow cooker. Push gently to make an even layer.
2. Layer rest of ingredients on top in order given.
3. Cover and cook on Low for 2–3 hours, until cheese is melted and spread is hot throughout.

Serve as a spread on crackers or thin slices of Italian bread or toast.

Colorful Fruit Salsa

JOYCE SHACKELFORD, GREEN BAY, WI

Makes 8–10 servings

Prep. Time: 25 minutes ❧ *Cooking Time: 2 hours*

Ideal slow-cooker size: 3-quart

- 11-oz. can mandarin oranges
- 8½-oz. can sliced peaches in juice, undrained
- 8-oz. can pineapple tidbits in juice, undrained
- 1 medium onion, chopped finely
- ½ cup finely chopped green bell pepper
- ½ cup finely chopped red bell pepper
- 1 jalapeño pepper, chopped finely
- 3 cloves garlic, minced
- 3 Tbsp. cornstarch
- 1 tsp. salt
- Juice of 1 lime
- Zest of 1 lime, cut in fine strips (not finely grated)
- ¼ cup chopped fresh cilantro
- Tortilla chips, for serving

1. Combine fruits, onion, peppers, garlic, cornstarch, and salt in slow cooker.
2. Cover and cook on High for 2 hours, stirring once each hour. Salsa should be thick and steaming, with the peppers softened.
3. Add lime juice and zest. Add cilantro. Remove salsa from slow cooker to a serving dish. Allow to cool for about 15 minutes before serving with tortilla chips.

Peach Chutney

JAN MAST, LANCASTER, PA

Makes 8 cups

Prep. Time: 10 minutes *Cooking Time: 5–8 hours*

Ideal slow-cooker size: 4-quart

2 (29-oz.) cans (about 6 cups) peaches, diced

1 cup raisins

1 small onion, chopped

1 clove garlic, minced

1 Tbsp. mustard seed

1 tsp. chopped dried red chilies

¼ cup chopped crystallized ginger

1 tsp. salt

¾ cup vinegar

½ cup brown sugar

1. Combine all ingredients in slow cooker.
2. Cover. Cook on Low 4–6 hours.
3. Remove lid. Stir chutney. Cook on High, uncovered, an additional 1–2 hours.

Venetian Stuffed Mushrooms

Marjanita Geigley, Lancaster, PA

Makes 8 servings

Prep. Time: 30 minutes *Cooking Time: 1½–2 hours*

Ideal slow-cooker size: Oval 6- to 7-quart

24 mushrooms, rinsed

2 Tbsp. olive oil

1 clove garlic

¼ tsp. butter

¼ cup shredded mozzarella cheese

2 Tbsp. Italian bread crumbs

2 tsp. Italian seasoning

¾ tsp. sea salt

¼ tsp. pepper

1. Remove stems from mushroom caps, including the piece of stem inside the cap.
2. Chop up stems.
3. Brush caps with oil and place them in slow cooker, cap side down.
4. Cook stems in garlic and butter until softened in a saucepan.
5. Stir in shredded cheese, bread crumbs, Italian seasoning, sea salt, and pepper.
6. Spoon the mushroom stem mixture into the caps.
7. Cover and cook on Low for 1½–2 hours.

Soups, Stews & Chilis

Shredded Pork Tortilla Soup

HOPE COMERFORD, CLINTON TOWNSHIP, MI

Makes 6–8 servings

Prep. Time: 10 minutes *Cooking Time: 8–10 hours*
Ideal slow-cooker size: 5-quart

3 large tomatoes, chopped
1 cup chopped red onion
1 jalapeño, seeded and minced
1 lb. pork loin
2 tsp. cumin
2 tsp. chili powder
2 tsp. onion powder
2 tsp. garlic powder
2 tsp. lime juice
8 cups chicken broth

garnish (optional):
fresh chopped cilantro
tortilla chips
avocado slices
freshly grated Mexican cheese

1. In your crock, place the tomatoes, onion, and jalapeño.
2. Place the pork loin on top.
3. Add all the seasonings and lime juice, and pour in the chicken broth.
4. Cover and cook on Low for 8–10 hours.
5. Remove the pork and shred it between two forks. Place it back into the soup and stir.
6. Serve each bowl of soup with fresh chopped cilantro, tortilla chips, avocado slices, and freshly grated Mexican cheese, if desired . . . or any other garnishes you would like!

TIP

If you don't have time for freshly chopped tomatoes, use a can of diced or chopped tomatoes.

Creamy Tomato Soup

SUSIE SHENK WENGER, LANCASTER, PA

Makes 4 servings

Prep. Time: 10–15 minutes *Cooking Time: 3–4 hours*

Ideal slow-cooker size: 3-quart

- 29-oz. can tomato sauce, or crushed tomatoes, or 1 quart home-canned tomatoes, chopped
- 1 small onion, chopped
- 1–2 carrots, sliced thin
- 2 tsp. brown sugar
- 1 tsp. Italian seasoning
- ¼ tsp. salt
- ¼ tsp. pepper
- 1 tsp. freshly chopped parsley
- ½ tsp. Worcestershire sauce
- 1 cup heaving whipping cream
- croutons, preferably homemade
- freshly grated Parmesan cheese

1. Combine tomato sauce, onion, carrots, brown sugar, Italian seasoning, salt, pepper, parsley, and Worcestershire sauce in slow cooker.
2. Cover. Cook on Low 3–4 hours, or until vegetables are soft.
3. Cool soup a bit. Puree with immersion blender.
4. Add cream and blend lightly again.
5. Serve hot with croutons and Parmesan as garnish.

Turkey Meatball Soup

MARY ANN LEFEVER, LANCASTER, PA

Makes 8 servings

Prep. Time: 30 minutes *Cooking Time: 8 hours*

Ideal slow-cooker size: 5- to 6-quart

4–5 large carrots, chopped

10 cups chicken broth

¾ lb. escarole, washed and cut into bite-sized pieces

1 lb. ground turkey, uncooked

1 medium onion, chopped

2 large eggs, beaten

½ cup Italian bread crumbs

½ cup freshly grated Parmesan, plus more for serving

1 tsp. salt

¼ tsp. pepper

1. In slow cooker, combine carrots and broth.
2. Stir in escarole.
3. Cover. Cook on Low 4 hours.
4. Combine turkey, onion, eggs, bread crumbs, ½ cup Parmesan cheese, salt, and pepper in good-sized bowl. Mix well and shape into 1-inch balls. Drop carefully into soup.
5. Cover cooker. Cook on Low 4 more hours, or just until meatballs and vegetables are cooked through.
6. Serve hot sprinkled with extra Parmesan cheese.

TIP

If you wish, you can substitute 3 cups cut-up cooked turkey for the ground turkey meatballs.

Cider and Pork Stew

VERONICA SABO, SHELTON, CT

Makes 5 servings

Prep. Time: 15 minutes ❧ *Cooking Time: 7–9 hours*

Ideal slow-cooker size: 3½-quart

2 medium (about 1¼ lb.) sweet potatoes, peeled if you wish, and cut into ¾-inch pieces

3 small carrots, peeled and cut into ½-inch-thick slices

1 cup chopped onion

1–2-lb. boneless pork shoulder, cut into 1-inch cubes

1 large Granny Smith apple, peeled, cored, and coarsely chopped

¼ cup flour

¾ tsp. salt

½ tsp. dried sage

½ tsp. thyme

½ tsp. pepper

1 cup apple cider

1. Layer sweet potatoes, carrots, onions, pork, and apple in slow cooker.
2. Combine flour, salt, sage, thyme, and pepper in medium bowl.
3. Add cider to flour mixture. Stir until smooth.
4. Pour cider mixture over meat and vegetables in slow cooker.
5. Cover. Cook on Low 7–9 hours, or until meat and vegetables are tender.

Chicken Chili

SHARON MILLER, HOLMESVILLE, OH

Makes 6 servings

Prep. Time: 15 minutes *Cooking Time: 5–6 hours*

Ideal slow-cooker size: 4-quart

2 lb. boneless, skinless chicken breasts, cubed

2 Tbsp. butter

2 (14-oz.) cans diced tomatoes, undrained

15-oz. can red kidney beans, rinsed and drained

1 cup diced onion

1 cup diced red bell pepper

1–2 Tbsp. chili powder, according to your taste preference

1 tsp. cumin

1 tsp. dried oregano

Salt and pepper, to taste

1. In skillet on high heat, brown chicken cubes in butter until they have some browned edges. Place in greased slow cooker.
2. Pour one of the cans of tomatoes with its juice into skillet to get all the browned bits and butter. Scrape and pour into slow cooker.
3. Add rest of ingredients, including other can of tomatoes, to cooker.
4. Cook on Low for 5–6 hours.

TIP

You can serve this chili with shredded cheddar cheese and sour cream.

Pumpkin Black-Bean Turkey Chili

RHODA ATZEFF, HARRISBURG, PA

Makes 10–12 servings

Prep. Time: 20 minutes *Cooking Time: 7–8 hours*

Ideal slow-cooker size: 5-quart

1 cup chopped onions

1 cup chopped yellow bell peppers

3 garlic cloves, minced

2 Tbsp. oil

1½ tsp. dried oregano

1½–2 tsp. ground cumin

2 tsp. chili powder

2 15-oz. cans black beans, rinsed and drained

2½ cups chopped cooked turkey

16-oz. can pumpkin

14½-oz. can diced tomatoes

3 cups chicken broth

1. Sauté onions, peppers, and garlic in oil in skillet for 8 minutes, or until soft.
2. Stir in oregano, cumin, and chili powder. Cook 1 minute. Transfer to slow cooker.
3. Stir in remaining ingredients.
4. Cover. Cook on Low 7–8 hours.

TIP

Top with roasted pumpkin seeds.

Shrimp Chowder

JOANNE GOOD, WHEATON, IL

Makes 12 servings

Prep. Time: 25 minutes *Cooking Time: 7 hours*

Ideal slow-cooker size: 4-quart

1 medium onion, chopped

5 medium russet potatoes, peeled and cubed

1½ cups diced, pre-cooked ham

4–6 cups water

salt and pepper, to taste

2 lb. shrimp, peeled, deveined, and cooked

chowder option:

4 Tbsp. flour

1 cup heavy (whipping) cream

1. Place chopped onion in microwave-safe bowl and cook in microwave for 2 minutes on High.
2. Place onion, cubed potatoes, diced ham, and 4 cups water in slow cooker. (If you're making the chowder option, whisk 4 Tbsp. flour into the 4 cups water in bowl before adding to slow cooker.)
3. Cover and cook on Low for 7 hours, or until potatoes are softened. If soup base is thicker than you like, add up to 2 cups more water.
4. About 15–20 minutes before serving, turn heat to High and add shrimp. If making chowder, also add heavy cream. Cook until shrimp are hot, about 15 minutes.

TIP

You can serve this chili with shredded cheddar cheese and sour cream.

Kale Chowder

COLLEEN HEATWOLE, BURTON, MI

Makes 8 servings

Prep. Time: 30 minutes *Cooking Time: 6 hours*
Ideal slow-cooker size: 6-quart

8 cups chicken broth

1 bunch of kale, cleaned, stems removed, and chopped

2 lb. potatoes, peeled and diced

4 cloves garlic, minced

1 onion, diced

1 lb. cooked ham

½ tsp. pepper, or to taste

1. Combine all ingredients in slow cooker.
2. Cover and cook on Low 6 hours, or until vegetables are tender.

If you are using new potatoes, peeling is optional.

Main Dishes

Pot Roast

JUDITH MARTIN, LEBANON, PA

Makes 12–15 servings

Prep. Time: 5 minutes · *Cooking Time: 7–8 hours*
Ideal slow-cooker size: 4-quart

2 (2½-lb.) boneless beef chuck roasts

1 envelope ranch salad dressing mix

1 envelope Italian salad dressing mix

1 envelope brown gravy mix

½–1 cup water

1. Place chuck roasts in a slow cooker.
2. Combine rest of ingredients and pour over the roasts.
3. Cover and cook on low for 7–8 hours.

Turn the juice into a nice gravy. This roast is very good reheated and served over potatoes with the gravy.

Barbecue Sandwiches

PHYLLIS GOOD, LANCASTER, PA

Makes 14–18 servings

Prep. Time: 20–30 minutes · *Cooking Time: 5–10 hours*
Ideal slow-cooker size: 5-quart

3 cups chopped celery

1 cup chopped onions

1 cup ketchup

1 cup barbecue sauce

1 cup water

2 Tbsp. vinegar

2 Tbsp. Worcestershire sauce

¼ cup dark brown sugar

1 tsp. salt

½ tsp. pepper

3–4-lb. boneless chuck roast

14–18 hamburger buns (or use slider buns)

1. Combine all ingredients except roast and buns in slow cooker. When well mixed, put the roast in the cooker. Spoon sauce over top of it.
2. Cover. Cook on High 5–6 hours, or on Low 8–10 hours.
3. Using two forks, pull the meat apart until it's shredded. You can do this in the cooker, or lift it out and do it on a good-sized platter or in a bowl.
4. Stir shredded meat into sauce. Turn the cooker to High if you're ready to eat soon. Or if it will be a while until mealtime, turn the cooker to Low. You're just making sure that the meat and sauce are heated through completely.
5. Serve on buns.

Orange Garlic Chicken

SUSAN KASTING, JENKS, OK

Makes 6 servings

Prep. Time: 15 minutes · *Cooking Time: 2½–6 hours*

Ideal slow-cooker size: 4-quart

1½ tsp. dried thyme

6 cloves garlic, minced

6 skinless bone-in chicken breast halves

1 cup orange juice concentrate

2 Tbsp. balsamic vinegar

1. Rub thyme and garlic over chicken. (Reserve any leftover thyme and garlic.) Place chicken in slow cooker.
2. Mix orange juice concentrate and vinegar together in a small bowl. Stir in reserved thyme and garlic. Spoon over chicken.
3. Cover and cook on Low 5–6 hours, or on High 2½–3 hours, or until chicken is tender but not dry.

Serve with mashed potatoes, cranberry sauce, and stuffing.

Balsamic Chicken

HOPE COMERFORD, CLINTON TOWNSHIP, MI

Makes 6 servings

Prep. Time: 10 minutes   *Cooking Time: 5–6 hours*

Ideal slow-cooker size: 3-quart

- 2 lb. boneless, skinless chicken breasts
- 2 Tbsp. olive oil
- ½ tsp. salt
- ½ tsp. pepper
- 1 onion, halved and sliced
- 28-oz. can diced tomatoes
- ½ cup balsamic vinegar
- 2 tsp. sugar
- 2 tsp. garlic powder
- 2 tsp. Italian seasoning
- cooked pasta for serving

1. Place chicken in crock. Drizzle with olive oil and sprinkle with salt and pepper.
2. Spread the onion over the top of the chicken.
3. In a bowl, mix together the diced tomatoes, balsamic vinegar, sugar, garlic powder, and Italian seasoning. Pour this over the chicken and onions.
4. Cover and cook on Low for 5–6 hours.
5. Serve over cooked pasta.

Slow Cooker Creamy Italian Chicken

SHERRI GRINDLE, GOSHEN, IN

Makes 8 servings

Prep. Time: 10–15 minutes *Cooking Time: 5–6 hours*

Ideal slow-cooker size: 4- to 5-quart

- 8 boneless, skinless chicken breast halves
- 1 envelope dry Italian salad dressing mix
- ¼ cup water
- 8-oz. pkg. cream cheese, softened
- 10¾-oz. can cream of chicken soup
- 4-oz. can mushrooms, drained

1. Place chicken in greased slow cooker.
2. Combine salad dressing mix and water in bowl. Pour over chicken.
3. Cover. Cook on Low 4–5 hours.
4. In saucepan, combine cream cheese and soup. Heat slightly to melt cream cheese. Stir in mushrooms. Pour over chicken.
5. Cover. Cook 1 additional hour on Low.

Serve over noodles or rice. Add frozen vegetables along with the mushrooms in Step 4, if desired.

Sweet Islands Chicken

CYNTHIA MORRIS, GROTTOES, VA

Makes 6 servings

Prep. Time: 15–20 minutes ❦ *Cooking Time: 3–4 hours*
Ideal slow-cooker size: 4-quart

1 cup pineapple juice

½ cup brown sugar

⅓ cup soy sauce

2 lb. boneless, skinless chicken thighs, cut in 1-inch chunks

1 Tbsp., plus 1 tsp., cornstarch

1. Grease interior of slow-cooker crock.
2. Mix pineapple juice, brown sugar, and soy sauce together in crock until well combined.
3. Stir in chicken chunks.
4. Cover. Cook on Low 3–4 hours, or until meat is cooked in center, but not dry.
5. When done cooking, spoon 1 Tbsp. and 1 tsp. sauce out of cooker and allow to cool in a small bowl.
6. Stir cornstarch into cooled sauce until smooth.
7. Stir cornstarch-sauce mix back into hot sauce remaining in crock. Continue stirring until sauce thickens.

Serve chicken and sauce over cooked rice or noodles.

Chicken and Dumplings

BONNIE MILLER, LOUISVILLE, OH

Makes 4 servings

Prep. Time: 20 minutes · *Cooking Time: 3–8 hours*

Ideal slow-cooker size: 4-quart

2 lbs. boneless, skinless chicken breast halves

1¾ cups chicken broth

2 chicken bouillon cubes

2 tsp. salt

1 tsp. pepper

1 tsp. poultry seasoning

2 celery ribs, cut into 1-inch pieces

6 small carrots, cut into 1-inch chunks

Biscuits:

2 cups buttermilk biscuit mix

½ cup plus 1 Tbsp. milk

1 tsp. parsley

1. Arrange chicken in slow cooker.
2. Dissolve bouillon in broth in bowl. Stir in salt, pepper, and poultry seasoning.
3. Pour over chicken.
4. Spread celery and carrots over top.
5. Cover. Cook on Low 6–8 hours or on High 3–3½ hours, or until chicken is tender but not dry.
6. Combine biscuit ingredients in a bowl until just moistened. Drop by spoonfuls over steaming chicken.
7. Cover. Cook on High 35 minutes. Do not remove cover while dumplings are cooking. Serve immediately.

Traditional Turkey Breast

HOPE COMERFORD, CLINTON TOWNSHIP, MI

Makes 10–12 servings

Prep. Time: 10 minutes *Cooking Time: 8 hours*

Ideal slow-cooker size: 7-quart

7-lb. or less turkey breast

olive oil

½ stick butter

Rub:

2 tsp. garlic powder

1 tsp. onion powder

1 tsp. salt

¼ tsp. pepper

1 tsp. poultry seasoning

1. Remove gizzards from turkey breast, rinse it, and pat dry. Place breast into crock.
2. Rub turkey breast all over with olive oil.
3. Cut the butter into 8 pieces. Mix together all rub ingredients. Rub this mixture all over turkey breast and press it in.
4. Place the pieces of butter all over top of the breast.
5. Cover and cook on Low for 8 hours.

Spicy Pulled Pork Sandwiches

JANIE STEELE, MOORE, OK

Makes 8–10 servings

Prep. Time: 20 minutes · *Cooking Time: 8½–10½ hours*

Ideal slow-cooker size: 5-quart

4-lb. pork loin

14 oz. low-sodium beef broth

⅓ cup Worcestershire sauce

⅓ cup Louisiana Hot Sauce

kaiser rolls or buns of your choice

Sauce:

½ cup Worcestershire sauce

¼ cup hot sauce

1 cup ketchup

1 cup molasses

½ cup mustard

1. Cut roast in half and place in slow cooker.
2. Mix broth, Worcestershire sauce, and hot sauce in a bowl and add to crock.
3. Cover and cook 8–10 hours on Low. Remove meat, discard liquid.
4. Shred pork loin with two forks and return to slow cooker. Mix sauce and pour over meat and mix.
5. Cover and cook 30 minutes more or until heated through. Serve on buns.

Simple Shredded Pork Tacos

JENNIFER FREED, ROCKINGHAM, AL

Makes 6 servings

Prep. Time: 5 minutes ❦ *Cooking Time: 8 hours*

Ideal slow-cooker size: 4-quart

- 2-lb. boneless pork roast
- 1 cup salsa
- 4-oz. can chopped green chilies
- ½ tsp. garlic salt
- ½ tsp. black pepper
- taco shells
- salsa, sour cream, or other favorite toppings

1. Place first five ingredients in slow cooker.
2. Cover; cook on Low 8 hours, or until meat is tender.
3. To serve, use 2 forks to shred pork. Layer on taco shells with favorite toppings.

Barbecued Ribs

VIRGINIA BENDER, DOVER, DE

Makes 6 servings

Prep. Time: 10 minutes *Cooking Time: 8–10 hours*
Ideal slow-cooker size: 6-quart

4 lb. pork ribs
½ cup brown sugar
12-oz. jar chili sauce
¼ cup balsamic vinegar
2 Tbsp. Worcestershire sauce
2 Tbsp. Dijon mustard
1 tsp. hot sauce

1. Place ribs in slow cooker.
2. Combine remaining ingredients in a good-sized bowl.
3. Pour half of sauce over ribs.
4. Cover. Cook on Low 8–10 hours.
5. Serve with remaining sauce.

Peppercorn Beef Roast

STACIE SKELLY, MILLERSVILLE, PA

Makes 6–8 servings

Prep. Time: 10–15 minutes ❦ *Cooking Time: 8–10 hours*

Ideal slow-cooker size: 4-quart

3–4-lb. chuck roast

½ cup gluten-free, reduced-sodium soy sauce or liquid aminos

1 tsp. garlic powder

1 bay leaf

3–4 peppercorns

2 cups water

1 tsp. thyme, optional

1. Place roast in the slow cooker.
2. In a mixing bowl, combine all other ingredients and pour over roast.
3. Cover and cook on Low 8–10 hours.
4. Remove meat to a platter and allow to rest before slicing or shredding.

TIP

To make gravy to go with the meat, whisk together ½ cup of gluten-free flour and ½ cup water, stir into meat juices in crock, turn cooker to High, and bring cooking juices to a boil until gravy is thickened.

Cheese-Stuffed Pizza

PHYLLIS GOOD, LANCASTER, PA

Makes 6 servings

Prep. Time: 30 minutes ✿ *Standing Time: 20 minutes* ✿ *Cooking Time: 2 hours*
Ideal slow-cooker size: 5-quart

- 11- or 13-oz. pkg. refrigerated pizza dough
- 1½ cups shredded mozzarella, divided
- ½ cup thick pizza sauce
- 1 cup or less favorite pizza toppings such as chopped vegetables or cooked meat

1. Divide dough in half. Roll and/or stretch each piece of dough into an oval to match the size of the bottom of the crock.
2. Place 1 dough oval in greased slow cooker, pushing and stretching it out to the edges. Sprinkle with ½ cup mozzarella.
3. Place the other dough oval on top of the cheese, stretching it to the edges of the crock.
4. Cook, uncovered, for 1 hour on High. Dough should be puffy and getting brown at edges.
5. Spread pizza sauce on top. Sprinkle with remaining 1 cup cheese and any toppings you wish.
6. Place lid on cooker with chopstick or wooden spoon handle to vent it at one end.
7. Cook on High for an additional hour, until toppings are heated through.

Easy Mac 'n' Cheese

JUANITA WEAVER, JOHNSONVILLE, IL

Makes 6 servings

Prep. Time: 5 minutes · *Cooking Time: 1½–2 hours*

Ideal slow-cooker size: 4½-quart

- 2 cups dry macaroni
- 4 cups milk
- 1 tsp. salt
- a pinch or two of black pepper
- 4 oz. cream cheese
- 8 slices of American or cheddar cheese
- ½ tsp. dry mustard or 1 tsp. prepared mustard
- 2 Tbsp. butter
- 4 slices of ham, cut into squares, optional

1. Measure all ingredients into slow cooker.
2. Turn cooker on High.
3. Cover and cook for 30 minutes, then stir lightly to evenly distribute cheeses.
4. Cook for another hour or so.

Veggies & Sides

Collard Greens with Bacon

HOPE COMERFORD, CLINTON TOWNSHIP, MI

Makes 8–10 servings

Prep. Time: 15 minutes · *Cooking Time: 5–6 hours*
Ideal slow-cooker size: 3-quart

- 3 lb. collard greens, tough stems cut away and washed thoroughly
- 8 oz. bacon, cooked, chopped
- 1½ cups chopped onion
- 4–5 cloves garlic, chopped
- 1 cup chicken stock
- 1 cup chopped tomatoes
- 3 Tbsp. apple cider vinegar
- 2 tsp. sea salt
- ¼ tsp. pepper
- 1 tsp. sugar
- 1 bay leaf

1. Tear the collard greens into large pieces and place in the crock.
2. Place all of the remaining ingredients in the crock and stir.
3. Cover and cook on Low for 5–6 hours.

Best Baked Beans

NADINE MARTINITZ, SALINA, KS

Makes 8–10 servings

Prep. Time: 15 minutes *Cooking Time: 2–6 hours*
Ideal slow-cooker size: 6-quart

8 strips bacon, diced

1 small onion, chopped

5 15-oz. cans pork and beans

2 Tbsp. Worcestershire sauce

⅓ cup brown sugar

½ cup molasses

½ cup ketchup

dash ground cloves

1. Sauté bacon in skillet until crisp. Remove bacon but retain drippings in skillet.
2. Brown chopped onion in drippings until translucent.
3. Combine all ingredients in slow cooker. Stir well.
4. Cover. Cook on Low 5–6 hours, or on High 2–3 hours.

Dilly Mashed Potatoes with Spinach

PHYLLIS GOOD, LANCASTER, PA

Makes 6–8 servings

Prep. Time: 25 minutes *Cooking Time: 4–6 hours and then 3–4 hours*
Ideal slow-cooker size: 5-quart

- 6 medium-sized potatoes
- 1 cup water
- 1 cup sour cream, or Greek yogurt, at room temperature
- 5 Tbsp. butter, at room temperature
- 4 oz. cream cheese, at room temperature
- 1¼ tsp. dill weed
- 1½ tsp. salt
- ⅛ tsp. pepper
- 2 spring onions, chopped
- 10-oz. box frozen chopped spinach, thawed and squeezed dry

1. Peel some or all of the potatoes. Cube. Place in slow cooker with water.
2. Cover and cook on Low for 4–6 hours, until potatoes are tender. Drain.
3. Place potatoes in mixing bowl. Add sour cream or yogurt, butter, cream cheese, dill, salt, and pepper.
4. Whip well with electric mixer.
5. Fold in spring onions and spinach.
6. Place mixture in lightly greased slow cooker, smoothing top.
7. Cook on Low for 3–4 hours.

Glazed Carrots

BARBARA SMITH, BEDFORD, PA

Makes 3–4 servings

Prep. Time: 15 minutes *Cooking Time: 2½–3½ hours*
Ideal slow-cooker size: 2½-quart

3 cups thinly sliced carrots or baby carrots

2 cups water

¼ tsp. salt

2–3 Tbsp. butter

3 Tbsp. orange marmalade

2 Tbsp. chopped pecans, optional

1. Combine carrots, water, and salt in slow cooker.
2. Cover. Cook on High 2–3 hours, or until carrots are as tender as you like them.
3. Drain. Stir in butter and marmalade.
4. Cover. Cook on High 30 minutes.
5. Sprinkle with chopped pecans before serving.

Eggplant Italian

MELANIE THROWER, MCPHERSON, KS

Makes 6–8 servings

Prep. Time: 30 minutes · *Cooking Time: 4 hours*

Ideal slow-cooker size: 4- or 5-quart oval

- 2 eggplants
- ¼ cup Egg Beaters
- 24 oz. fat-free cottage cheese
- ¼ tsp. salt
- black pepper to taste
- 14-oz. can tomato sauce
- 2–4 Tbsp. Italian seasoning, according to your taste preference

1. Peel eggplants and cut in ½-inch thick slices. Soak in salt water for about 5 minutes to remove bitterness. Drain well.
2. Spray slow cooker with fat-free cooking spray.
3. Mix Egg Beaters, cottage cheese, salt, and pepper together in bowl.
4. Mix tomato sauce and Italian seasoning together in another bowl.
5. Spoon a thin layer of tomato sauce into bottom of slow cooker. Top with about one-third of eggplant slices, and then one-third of egg/cheese mixture, and finally one-third of remaining tomato sauce mixture.
6. Repeat those layers twice, ending with seasoned tomato sauce.
7. Cover. Cook on High 4 hours. Allow to rest 15 minutes before serving.

Desserts

Dates in Cardamom Coffee Syrup

MARGARET W. HIGH, LANCASTER, PA

Makes 12 servings

Prep. Time: 15 minutes *Cooking Time: 7–8 hours*

Ideal slow-cooker size: 3-quart

2 cups pitted, whole, dried dates

2½ cups very strong, hot brewed coffee

2 Tbsp. turbinado sugar

15 whole green cardamom pods

4-inch cinnamon stick

plain Greek yogurt, for serving

1. Combine dates, coffee, sugar, cardamom, and cinnamon stick in the slow cooker.
2. Cover and cook on High for 1 hour. Remove lid and continue to cook on High for 6–7 hours until sauce has reduced.
3. Pour dates and sauce into container and chill in fridge.
4. To serve, put a scoop of Greek yogurt in a small dish and add a few dates on top. Drizzle with a little sauce.

Sour Cherry Cobbler

MARGARET W. HIGH, LANCASTER, PA

Makes 6–8 servings

Prep. Time: 20 minutes · *Cooking Time: 2 hours*

Ideal slow-cooker size: 6-quart

- ½ cup whole wheat flour
- ¾ cup all-purpose flour, divided
- 1 Tbsp. sugar, plus ⅔ cup sugar, divided
- 1 tsp. baking powder
- ¼ tsp. salt
- ¼ tsp. ground cinnamon
- ¼ tsp. almond extract
- 1 egg
- ¼ cup milk
- 2 Tbsp. melted butter
- 4 cups pitted sour cherries, thawed and drained if frozen

1. In mixing bowl, combine whole wheat flour and ½ cup all-purpose flour. Mix in 1 Tbsp. sugar, baking powder, salt, and cinnamon.
2. Separately, combine almond extract, egg, milk, and butter. Stir into dry ingredients just until moistened.
3. Spread batter in bottom of greased slow cooker.
4. Separately, mix remaining ¼ cup flour with ⅔ cup sugar. Add cherries. Sprinkle cherry mixture evenly over batter in slow cooker.
5. Cover and cook on High 2 hours or until lightly browned at edges and juice is bubbling from cherries.

TIP

Cobblers are wonderful served warm with vanilla ice cream, whipped cream, or custard sauce.

Chocolate Pudding Cake

SARAH HERR, GOSHEN, IN

Makes 8 servings

Prep. Time: 15 minutes ❧ *Cooking Time: 2–3 hours*

Ideal slow-cooker size: 3½-quart

- 1 cup dry all-purpose baking mix
- 1 cup sugar, divided
- 3 Tbsp. unsweetened cocoa powder, plus ⅓ cup, divided
- ½ cup milk
- 1 tsp. vanilla extract
- 1⅔ cups hot water

1. Spray inside of slow cooker with nonstick cooking spray.
2. In a bowl, mix together baking mix, ½ cup sugar, 3 Tbsp. cocoa powder, milk, and vanilla. Spoon batter evenly into slow cooker.
3. In a clean bowl, mix remaining ½ cup sugar, ⅓ cup cocoa powder, and hot water together. Pour over batter in slow cooker. Do not stir.
4. Cover and cook on High 2–3 hours, or until toothpick inserted in center of cakey part comes out clean.

The batter will rise to the top and turn into cake. Underneath will be a rich chocolate pudding.

Peanut Butter and Hot Fudge Cake

SARA WILSON, BLAIRSTOWN, MO

Makes 6 servings

Prep. Time: 10 minutes · *Cooking Time: 2–3 hours*

Ideal slow-cooker size: 4-quart

½ cup flour

¾ cup sugar, divided

¾ tsp. baking powder

⅓ cup milk

1 Tbsp. oil

½ tsp. vanilla extract

¼ cup peanut butter

3 Tbsp. unsweetened cocoa powder

1 cup boiling water

1. Combine flour, ¼ cup sugar, and baking powder. Add milk, oil, and vanilla. Mix until smooth. Stir in peanut butter. Pour into slow cooker.
2. Mix together ½ cup sugar and cocoa powder. Gradually stir in boiling water. Pour mixture over batter in slow cooker. Do not stir.
3. Cover and cook on High 2–3 hours, or until toothpick inserted comes out clean.

TIP

Serve warm and with vanilla ice cream.

Mama's Rice Pudding

DONNA BARNITZ, JENKS, OK
SHARI JENSEN, FOUNTAIN, CO

Makes 4–6 servings

Prep. Time: 5 minutes · *Cooking Time: 6–7 hours*

Ideal slow-cooker size: 4-quart

- ½ cup white rice, uncooked
- ½ cup sugar
- 1 tsp. vanilla extract
- 1 tsp. lemon extract
- 1 cup plus 2 Tbsp. milk
- 1 tsp. butter
- 2 eggs, beaten
- 1 tsp. cinnamon
- ½ cup raisins
- 1 cup whipping cream whipped
- nutmeg

1. Combine all ingredients except whipped cream and nutmeg in slow cooker. Stir well.
2. Cover pot. Cook on Low 6–7 hours, until rice is tender and milk absorbed. Be sure to stir once every 2 hours during cooking.
3. Pour into bowl. Cover with plastic wrap and chill.
4. Before serving, fold in whipped cream and sprinkle with nutmeg.

Seven Layer Bars

MARY W. STAUFFER, EPHRATA, PA

Makes 6–8 servings

Prep. Time: 5–10 minutes *Cooking Time: 2–3 hours*

Ideal slow-cooker size: 4 to 5-quart

¼ cup melted butter

½ cup graham cracker crumbs

½ cup chocolate chips

½ cup butterscotch chips

½ cup flaked coconut

½ cup chopped nuts

½ cup sweetened condensed milk

1. Layer ingredients in a bread or cake pan that fits in your slow cooker, in the order listed. Do not stir.
2. Cover and bake on High 2–3 hours, or until firm. Remove pan and uncover. Let stand 5 minutes.
3. Unmold carefully on plate and cool.

Baked Apples

MARLENE WEAVER, LITITZ, PA

Makes 4–6 servings

Prep. Time: 10 minutes   *Cooking Time: 4 hours*

Ideal slow-cooker size: 6-quart

2 Tbsp. raisins

¼ cup sugar

6–8 baking apples, cored

1 tsp. cinnamon

2 Tbsp. butter

½ cup water

1. Mix raisins and sugar; fill center of apples.
2. Sprinkle with cinnamon and dot with butter.
3. Place in slow cooker; add water.
4. Cover and cook on Low for 4 hours.

Unbelievable Carrot Cake

PHYLLIS GOOD, LANCASTER, PA

Makes 12–14 servings

Prep. Time: 15 minutes *Cooking Time: 3½–4 hours*
Ideal slow-cooker size: 6- or 7-quart oval

2-layer spice cake mix

2 cups (½ lb.) shredded carrots

1 cup crushed pineapple with juice

3 egg whites

½ cup All-Bran cereal

Cream Cheese Frosting:

3-oz. pkg. cream cheese, softened

4 Tbsp. (half a stick) butter, softened

2 cups confectioners' sugar

vanilla milk (start with 1 Tbsp. and increase gradually if you need more)

1. Combine the dry cake mix, shredded carrots, crushed pineapple with juice, egg whites, and All-Bran cereal thoroughly in a big bowl.
2. Grease and flour a loaf pan.
3. Pour batter into prepared pan.
4. Cover with greased foil and place in slow cooker.
5. Cover cooker with its lid.
6. Bake on High for 3½–4 hours, or until tester inserted in center of cake comes out clean.
7. Carefully remove pan from cooker. Place on wire baking rack to cool, uncovered.
8. As the cake cools, make the frosting by mixing together the softened cream cheese and butter, confectioners' sugar, and vanilla. When well combined, stir in milk, starting with 1 Tbsp. and adding more if necessary, until the frosting becomes spreadable.
9. Frost cake when it's completely cooled.
10. Slice and serve.

No need to shred carrots if you don't have time. You can buy them already shredded! Also, if you don't have time to make your own frosting, there is no shame in purchasing pre-made frosting for this delicious cake!

Harvest Goodie

MARJANITA GEIGLEY, LANCASTER, PA

Makes 5–6 servings

Prep. Time: 30 minutes *Cooking Time: 2–4 hours*

Ideal slow-cooker size: 4-quart

- 2 cups sliced apples
- 2 cups sliced peaches
- ¾ cup brown sugar
- ½ cup flour
- ½ cup oats
- ⅓ cup softened butter
- ¾ tsp. cinnamon
- ¾ tsp. nutmeg

1. Spray or grease slow cooker.
2. Place in mixed apples and peaches.
3. Mix other ingredients together and pour over top of fruit.
4. Cook on Low for 2–4 hours.

TIP

Serve warm and with vanilla-bean ice cream or a cold glass of milk.

Easy Chocolate Clusters

MARCELLA STALTER, FLANAGAN, IL

Makes 3½ dozen clusters

Prep. Time: 5 minutes ⁂ *Cooking Time: 2 hours*

Ideal slow-cooker size: 4-quart

- 2 lb. white coating chocolate, broken into small pieces
- 2 cups semisweet chocolate chips
- 4-oz. pkg. sweet German chocolate
- 24-oz. jar roasted peanuts

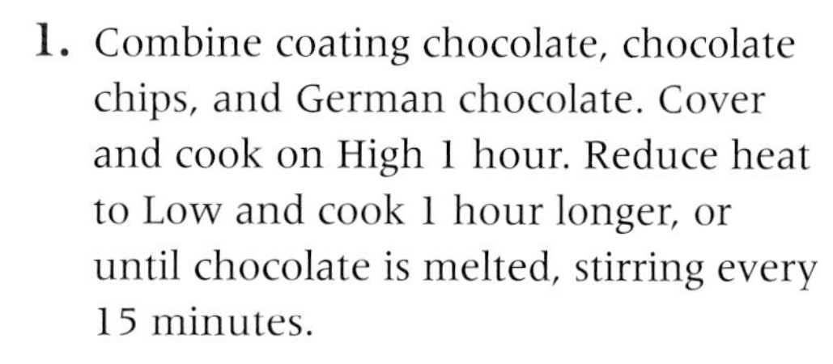

1. Combine coating chocolate, chocolate chips, and German chocolate. Cover and cook on High 1 hour. Reduce heat to Low and cook 1 hour longer, or until chocolate is melted, stirring every 15 minutes.
2. Stir in peanuts. Mix well.
3. Drop by teaspoonfuls onto waxed paper. Let stand until set. Store at room temperature.

Try these with cashews in place of the peanuts.

Bold Butterscotch Sauce

MARGARET W. HIGH, LANCASTER, PA

Makes 16 servings

Prep. Time: 10 minutes *Cooking Time: 2–3 hours*

Ideal slow-cooker size: 3-quart

8 Tbsp. (1 stick) salted butter

1 cup dark brown sugar, packed

1 cup heavy cream

½ tsp. salt, or more to taste

2 tsp. vanilla extract, or more to taste

1. Cut butter in slices. Add to heatproof bowl that will fit in your slow cooker.
2. Add sugar, cream, and salt.
3. Add water to crock and place bowl with butter mixture in crock so that water comes halfway up its sides.
4. Cover and cook on High for 2–3 hours, until sauce is steaming hot.
5. Wearing oven mitts to protect your knuckles, remove hot bowl from cooker.
6. Add vanilla. Stir. Taste. Add more vanilla and/or salt to achieve a bold butterscotch flavor.

TIP

Store butterscotch in lidded jar in fridge for several weeks. Warm and stir before serving.

Metric Equivalent Measurements

If you're accustomed to using metric measurements, I don't want you to be inconvenienced by the imperial measurements I use in this book.

Use this handy chart, too, to figure out the size of the slow cooker you'll need for each recipe.

Weight (Dry Ingredients)

1 oz		30 g
4 oz	¼ lb	120 g
8 oz	½ lb	240 g
12 oz	¾ lb	360 g
16 oz	1 lb	480 g
32 oz	2 lb	960 g

Slow Cooker Sizes

1-quart	0.96 l
2-quart	1.92 l
3-quart	2.88 l
4-quart	3.84 l
5-quart	4.80 l
6-quart	5.76 l
7-quart	6.72 l
8-quart	7.68 l

Volume (Liquid Ingredients)

½ tsp.		2 ml
1 tsp.		5 ml
1 Tbsp.	½ fl oz	15 ml
2 Tbsp.	1 fl oz	30 ml
¼ cup	2 fl oz	60 ml
⅓ cup	3 fl oz	80 ml
½ cup	4 fl oz	120 ml
⅔ cup	5 fl oz	160 ml
¾ cup	6 fl oz	180 ml
1 cup	8 fl oz	240 ml
1 pt	16 fl oz	480 ml
1 qt	32 fl oz	960 ml

Length

¼ in	6 mm
½ in	13 mm
¾ in	19 mm
1 in	25 mm
6 in	15 cm
12 in	30 cm

Recipe and Ingredient Index

T

U

V

Y